Ch

by Iain Gray

Lang**Syne**

PUBLISHING

WRITING *to* REMEMBER

79 Main Street, Newtongrange,
Midlothian EH22 4NA
Tel: 0131 344 0414   Fax: 0845 075 6085
E-mail: info@lang-syne.co.uk
www.langsyneshop.co.uk

Design by Dorothy Meikle
Printed by Ricoh Print Scotland
© Lang Syne Publishers Ltd 2015

All rights reserved. No part of this publication may be reproduced, stored
or introduced into a retrieval system, or transmitted in any form or by any
means (electronic, mechanical, photocopying, recording or otherwise) without
the prior written permission of Lang Syne Publishers Ltd.

ISBN 978-1-85217-417-0

Christie

MOTTO:
Thus I Flourish.

CREST:
An oak tree sprouting new growth.

NAME variations include:
Christe
Christy
MacChristie
McChristie
MacChristy
McChristy

The spirit of the clan means much to thousands of people

Chapter one:

The origins of the clan system

by Rennie McOwan

The original Scottish clans of the Highlands and the great families of the Lowlands and Borders were gatherings of families, relatives, allies and neighbours for mutual protection against rivals or invaders.

Scotland experienced invasion from the Vikings, the Romans and English armies from the south. The Norman invasion of what is now England also had an influence on land-holding in Scotland. Some of these invaders stayed on and in time became 'Scottish'.

The word clan derives from the Gaelic language term 'clann', meaning children, and it was first used many centuries ago as communities were formed around tribal lands in glens and mountain fastnesses.

The format of clans changed over the centuries, but at its best the chief and his family held the land on behalf of all, like trustees, and the ordinary clansmen and women believed they had a blood relationship with the founder of their clan.

There were two way duties and obligations. An inadequate chief could be deposed and replaced by someone of greater ability.

Clan people had an immense pride in race. Their relationship with the chief was like adult children to a father and they had a real dignity.

The concept of clanship is very old and a more feudal notion of authority gradually crept in.

Pictland, for instance, was divided into seven principalities ruled by feudal leaders who were the strongest and most charismatic leaders of their particular groups.

By the sixth century the 'British' kingdoms of Strathclyde, Lothian and Celtic Dalriada (Argyll) had emerged and Scotland, as one nation, began to take shape in the time of King Kenneth MacAlpin.

Some chiefs claimed descent from ancient kings which may not have been accurate in every case.

By the twelfth and thirteenth centuries the clans and families were more strongly brought under the central control of Scottish monarchs.

Lands were awarded and administered more and more under royal favour, yet the power of the area clan chiefs was still very great.

The long wars to ensure Scotland's

independence against the expansionist ideas of English monarchs extended the influence of some clans and reduced the lands of others.

Those who supported Scotland's greatest king, Robert the Bruce, were awarded the territories of the families who had opposed his claim to the Scottish throne.

In the Scottish Borders country – the notorious Debatable Lands – the great families built up a ferocious reputation for providing warlike men accustomed to raiding into England and occasionally fighting one another.

Chiefs had the power to dispense justice and to confiscate lands and clan warfare produced a society where martial virtues – courage, hardiness, tenacity – were greatly admired.

Gradually the relationship between the clans and the Crown became strained as Scottish monarchs became more orientated to life in the Lowlands and, on occasion, towards England.

The Highland clans spoke a different language, Gaelic, whereas the language of Lowland Scotland and the court was Scots and in more modern times, English.

Highlanders dressed differently, had different

customs, and their wild mountain land sometimes seemed almost foreign to people living in the Lowlands.

It must be emphasised that Gaelic culture was very rich and story-telling, poetry, piping, the clarsach (harp) and other music all flourished and were greatly respected.

Highland culture was different from other parts of Scotland but it was not inferior or less sophisticated.

Central Government, whether in London or Edinburgh, sometimes saw the Gaelic clans as a challenge to their authority and some sent expeditions into the Highlands and west to crush the power of the Lords of the Isles.

Nevertheless, when the eighteenth century Jacobite Risings came along the cause of the Stuarts was mainly supported by Highland clans.

The word Jacobite comes from the Latin for James – Jacobus. The Jacobites wanted to restore the exiled Stuarts to the throne of Britain.

The monarchies of Scotland and England became one in 1603 when King James VI of Scotland (1st of England) gained the English throne after Queen Elizabeth died.

The Union of Parliaments of Scotland and England, the Treaty of Union, took place in 1707.

Some Highland clans, of course, and Lowland families opposed the Jacobites and supported the incoming Hanoverians.

After the Jacobite cause finally went down at Culloden in 1746 a kind of ethnic cleansing took place. The power of the chiefs was curtailed. Tartan and the pipes were banned in law.

Many emigrated, some because they wanted to, some because they were evicted by force. In addition, many Highlanders left for the cities of the south to seek work.

Many of the clan lands became home to sheep and deer shooting estates.

But the warlike traditions of the clans and the great Lowland and Border families lived on, with their descendants fighting bravely for freedom in two world wars.

Remember the men from whence you came, says the Gaelic proverb, and to that could be added the role of many heroic women.

The spirit of the clan, of having roots, whether Highland or Lowland, means much to thousands of people.

Chapter two:

On the field of battle

Ranked at 78th in the list of the 100 most popular surnames found in Scotland, the spelling form 'Christie' is of Scottish origin – and what it has in common with other variations of the name is that it derives from what from earliest times was the popular forename 'Christian.'

Indicating 'son of Christian', and first introduced to British shores in the wake of the Norman invasion of 1066, the Christie form of the name is now found throughout Scotland, although from earliest times it was particularly prevalent in Fife.

'Christy' is considered an Irish form of the name, indicating 'Christ' – and some sources assert this form may derive from the Danish 'cruset', meaning 'cup', and in support of this is the fact that a family of the name of Christy who flourished on the Isle of Man claimed a Danish ancestry.

In Scotland, meanwhile, many bearers of what remains today the popular name of Gilchrist are thought to have at some period adopted the name Christie.

Four prominent families of the Christie name, all with their own Coats of Arms, are known to have risen to prominence in the areas of present-day Fife, Aberdeen, Midlothian and Galloway, and one intriguing tradition asserts that some of them may have been of ancient Pictish origin.

This mysterious race, whose name is thought to have derived from accounts penned in Latin that described them as 'painted' or 'tattooed' people, flourished north of the rivers Forth and Clyde until about the eleventh century, by which time they had been amalgamated with the Gaels to form what later became the kingdom of Scotland.

One of the four Pictish sub-kingdoms was known as Fib, modern-day Fife, the very area in which bearers of the Christie name existed from earliest times, while the others were modern-day Moray, Angus and the Mearns and Atholl.

Whatever their ancient origin, what is known with certainty is that the Christies enjoyed a close kinship with Clan Farquharson – to the extent that, along with others who include the Barries, Finlays, Hardies, MacCartneys and Patersons, they are recognised as a sept, or sub-branch, of this distinguished Highland clan.

As such, although the Christies have their own proud motto of 'Thus I Flourish' and crest of an oak tree sprouting new growth, they are also entitled to share in the honours of the Farquharsons, whose motto is 'Fidelity and Fortitude' and crest a demi-lion holding a sword in its right paw.

As kinsfolk of the Farquharsons, whose name is derived from 'fear' and 'char', indicating 'dear one', the Christies for centuries shared in both their fortunes and misfortunes.

This clan to which the Christies were closely linked takes its name, known in Gaelic as Mac Fhearchair, from Farquhar Shaw, a son of Alexander Mackintosh of Rothiemurchus, the 5th Chief of Clan Shaw, and whose territory lay in the Braes of Mar, in Deeside.

It was after his son married Isobel Stewart, the heiress of Invercauld, near Braemar, that the chiefly line of the Farquharsons became more properly known as the Farquharsons of Invercauld.

Invercauld House remains the seat of the Clan Chief of the Farquharsons.

Farquhar Shaw's grandson, Finla Mor Farquharson, along with many of his clan and kinsfolk such as the Christies, were among those killed in 1547 in the battle of Pinkie, near Musselburgh, on Scotland's east coast.

The battle had followed the invasion of a 25,000-strong English army under the Duke of Somerset, and 3,000 clansmen and their kinsmen under the leadership of the Earl of Argyll were either killed on the battlefield or forced to flee to safety.

Nearly 50 years after the battle, the Farquharsons and their kinsfolk entered a bond with Clan Mackintosh, thus making them, along with others that included the MacPhersons, MacThomases of Finegand and the Davidsons, members of the mighty confederation of clans known as Clan Chattan.

As members of Clan Chattan – whose motto is 'Touch not the cat without a glove', and crest a rampant wildcat, the Farquharsons and their kinsfolk such as the Christies were loyal in their support of the Royal House of Stuart.

Following what is known as the Glorious Revolution of 1688 that brought William of Orange and his wife Mary to the thrones of England and Scotland, John Graham of Claverhouse, Viscount Dundee, raised the Royal Standard in favour of the exiled Stuart monarch James VII and II.

Gathering a 2,500-strong force of clansmen

that included a contingent under John Farquharson of Inverey, he engaged a 4000-strong government force under General Hugh Mackay of Scourie at the Pass of Killiecrankie on July 27, 1689.

Brave, but undisciplined, the clansmen fired off a volley of musket fire before throwing the muskets to the ground and rushing pell-mell down hill into Mackay's closely packed ranks.

The clansmen were mown down in their hundreds by the disciplined musket fire of Mackay's troopers, but not before inflicting equally heavy losses.

Both sides suffered terribly in the battle, with John Farquharson among the many dead, and the outcome proved to be inconclusive – while John Graham of Claverhouse died the next day from his wounds.

In the following century, the Farquharsons and their Christie kinsmen also fought for the cause of the Stuarts in the abortive Jacobite Risings of 1715 and 1745.

In later centuries and in much different conflicts, bearers of the Christie name gained honours and distinction.

During the terrible carnage of the First World War, John Christie, better known as Jock Christie, was a recipient of the Victoria Cross (VC), the highest

Christie 15

award for bravery in the face of enemy action for British and Commonwealth forces.

Born in 1895 in Edmonton, London, he had been a lance-corporal in the 1/11th (County of London) Battalion, The London Regiment (Finsbury Rifles), when in December of 1917 at Fejja, Palestine, as he and his comrades were in danger of being overrun by the enemy, he performed the actions that won him his VC.

He single-handedly carried a supply of grenades along a communications trench and, despite heavy opposition, launched a successful counter-attack by bombing the enemy; he died in 1967.

Two American bearers of the Christie name who made a significant contribution to Allied success during the Second World War were John Walter Christie, better known as J. Walter Christie, and Ralph Waldo Christie, better known as Ralph W. Christie.

Born in 1865 in New Milford, New Jersey, J. Walter Christie was the engineer and inventor who, in the early 1900s, was involved in front wheel drive designs for motor vehicles and who, in 1907, became the first American to compete in the French Grand Prix.

He also designed New York taxicabs, but it is

for his revolutionary suspension system for tanks that he is best known.

Known as the Christie suspension system, it was, ironically, not fully adopted by the U.S. Army during the Second World War because of bureaucratic wrangling – but was eagerly taken up by America's allies.

This resulted in the Soviet BT and famed T-34 series of tanks and the British Crusader and Covenanter series.

He died in 1944, a year before the end of the conflict in which his tank suspension system had played such a significant role.

From land war to the high seas, Ralph W. Christie, born in 1893 in Somerville, Massachusetts was the United States Navy admiral who played a key role in the development of torpedo technology.

Responsible for the development of the Mark 14 torpedo and the equally highly effective Mark IV magnetic exploder, he died in 1987, the recipient of honours that include the Navy Distinguished Service Medal, the Legion of Merit and the Silver Star.

Chapter three:

Politics and commerce

Far from the fields of conflict, bearers of the Christie name have stamped their mark on the historical record through a variety of other endeavours – not least in Canada, where many have been of Scottish stock.

Born in 1787 in Windsor, Nova Scotia, the son of a Scottish immigrant, Robert Christie was the lawyer, historian and journalist who became a leading political figure in Canada East and Lower Canada.

Elected in 1841 to the 1st Parliament of the Province of Canada, it was Christie who a year later introduced the motion to move the capital from Kingston to Montreal.

Editor of the *Quebec Mercury* newspaper from 1848 to 1850, he died in 1856.

Born in Edinburgh in 1818 and arriving in Canada with his family at the age of 15, David Christie also achieved high political office.

Elected to the Legislative Council of the Province of Canada in 1867, he later served in the Canadian Senate, representing Erie, Ontario.

Secretary of State for Canada from 1873 to 1874 and Speaker of the Senate from 1874 to 1878, he died in 1880.

Yet another Scot who pursued a successful career in Canadian politics was Thomas Christie, who was born in Glasgow in 1834.

Arriving in Lower Canada with his parents at the age of three, he later qualified in medicine from McGill University before representing Argenteuil, in Quebec, in the Canadian House of Commons from 1875 to 1880 and from 1891 to 1902.

He was succeeded as the Liberal representative for Argenteuil by his son, Thomas Christie, Jr., following his death in 1902.

Born in 1941, a grandson of the Scottish Presbyterian missionary and doctor Dr Dugald Christie, founder of the Mukden Medical College in Shenyang, China, Dugald Christie was the Canadian lawyer and leading political activist who campaigned for legal services for people on low incomes.

He began to offer free legal services to low-income people in Vancouver in 1991, and, as head of the Western Canada Society to Access Justice, he was responsible for the establishment of free legal clinics across the area.

It was in order to raise awareness of the shortcomings of Canada's legal assistance programmes that, in 2006, he embarked on a bicycle trip across the nation.

But tragedy struck during the trip when he was killed after being struck by a car in Sault Ste. Marie, Ontario.

One particularly enterprising bearer of the Christie name was William Mellis Christie, who was born in Huntly, Aberdeenshire, in 1829, and who is famed as the creator of the popular 'Mr Christie' brand of biscuits and cookies.

He apprenticed as a baker before immigrating to Canada in 1848 and later, along with Alexander Brown, co-founded the bakery in Toronto that by 1868 was known as Christie, Brown and Company.

By just over ten years later, it had become the largest manufacturer of biscuits in Canada and continued as a family concern until it was bought by Nabisco 28 years after Christie's death in 1910.

Toronto's Christie Street is named in his honour.

From Canada to the original Christie homeland of Scotland, Campbell Christie was the general secretary of the Scottish Trades Union Congress

(STUC) who was born in 1937 in Careluith, Dumfries and Galloway.

Moving to Glasgow with his family at the age of 12, he became active in trade unionism after joining the Civil Service and moving to London, becoming deputy general secretary of the Society of Civil and Public Servants in 1971.

Returning to Scotland in 1986, he became general secretary of the STUC, a post in which he served until his retirement in 1998.

Numerous other posts he held include STUC representative on the Scottish Constitutional Convention, the economic and social committee of the European Community, from 1992 until 1998, director of the Glasgow Development Agency and vice-chair of the board of British Waterways.

The recipient of honours that include a CBE, awarded in 1997, and honorary degrees from a number of Scottish universities and colleges, he was also a chairman of Falkirk Football Club; he died in 2011.

From Scotland to the much warmer climes of the Bahamas, Perry Christie, born in 1944 in Nassau, is the Progressive Liberal Party politician who, in addition to serving as Prime Minister of the Bahamas from 2002 to 2007, also, as an athlete, represented his nation at the 1960 West Indies Federation Games.

In the ecclesiastical realm, Alexander Christie, born in 1848 in Highgate, Vermont, was the American prelate of the Roman Catholic Church who served as Archbishop of Oregon from 1899 until his death in 1925.

In 1901 he also helped to found the University of Portland, Oregon, and, three years before his death, the Catholic Truth Society.

Returning again to Scotland, John Cairns Christie, born in 1947 in Glasgow, is the former science teacher, ordained as a minister in 1990, who served as Moderator of the General Assembly of the Church of Scotland from May 2010 to May 2011.

Chapter four:

On the world stage

In other spheres of endeavour, Julie Christie, born in 1941 in Assam, India, where her father ran a tea plantation, is the award-winning British actress who was also one of the icons of London's 'Swinging Sixties' era.

It was after studying at London's Central School of Speech and Drama that she first came to attention for her role in the 1961 British television science fiction series *'A' for Andromeda*.

This was quickly followed by a string of film successes that include the 1962 romantic comedy *The Fast Lady*, the 1963 *Billy Liar*, for which she received a BAFTA nomination for Best British Actress and the 1965 *Darling*, for which she received an Academy Award for Best Actress and a BAFTA for the same.

Other major film roles include *Doctor Zhivago*, from 1965, the 1967 *Far from the Madding Crowd*, the 1975 *Shampoo* and, from 1997, *Afterglow*, for which she received an Academy nomination for Best Actress.

Successful on stage in addition to film, she also appeared in a 1964 Broadway production of *The Comedy of Errors*.

A partner of American actor Warren Beatty for a time, she later married the British journalist Duncan Campbell.

Also on the stage, **Dick Christie** is the American actor and screenwriter born in 1948 in Long Beach, California.

Best known for his role in the 1980s as Ted Lawson in the television sitcom *Small Wonder*, he also wrote the screenplay for the 1998 film *Molly*.

Behind the camera lens, the Canadian brothers **Charles** and **Al Christie**, born in London, Ontario in, respectively, 1880 and 1881, were movie moguls of the 1920s.

Leaving Canada as young men for Hollywood and what was then its fledgling film industry, and working on a number of films, they accrued enough money to set up their own company, the Christie Film Company, on Hollywood Boulevard, specialising in comedy productions.

With Charles concentrating on the business side and his brother on production, direction and screenwriting, they soon became recognised as two of the most powerful figures in the Hollywood film industry.

One indication of their success was that in 1922 they built Hollywood's Christie Hotel, which boasted the then very rare luxury of en-suite bathrooms.

But, in common with many other businesses, the Christie Film Company was forced into receivership following the stock market collapse of 1929 and subsequent Great Depression.

Al Christie, who died in 1951, continued working for the company that took over the business he and his brother had set up, while Charles, who died in 1955, turned to selling real estate.

Both have stars on the Hollywood Walk of Fame in recognition of their contribution to the early film industry.

From film to the world of music, **Tony Christie** is the English singer and musician who was born Anthony Fitzgerald in 1943 in West Yorkshire.

Best known for the 1971 chart hits *I Did What I Did for Maria* and *Amarillo*, his *Avenues and Alleyways* was also used as the theme tune for the television series *The Protectors*.

Amarillo enjoyed renewed chart success in

2005 when it was re-released to raise money for the British Comic Relief Charity, while Christie was also awarded the freedom of Amarillo, in Texas, for helping to raise the city's international profile.

Also in contemporary popular music, **Lou Christie** is the American singer and songwriter who was born Lugee Alfredo Giovanni Sacco in Glenwillard, Pennsylvania, in 1943.

International hits he has enjoyed, featuring his distinctive falsetto, include the 1966 *Lightnin' Strikes* and the 1969 *I'm Gonna Make You Mine*.

In a different musical genre, **Keith Christie**, born in 1931 in Blackpool and who died in 1980, was the English jazz trombonist who, in addition to playing with the Ted Heath Orchestra from 1957 until the late 1960s, also played for artistes who included Johnny Dankworth, Cleo Laine and Tommy Whittle.

His brother, **Ian Christie**, born in 1927 and who died in 2010, was the jazz clarinettist and photographer who, in addition to playing in a number of traditional jazz ensembles in the 1950s, also worked for a number of years as a film critic for the *Daily Express* newspaper.

Born in 1882 in Eggesford, Devon, into a wealthy land-owning family, **John Christie** was the founder in 1934 of the internationally renowned Glyndebourne Opera House and the Glyndebourne Festival Opera, staged annually at the Christie family home in Glyndebourne, near Lewes, in Sussex.

He died in 1962, six years after being made a Companion of Honour for his achievement at Glyndebourne – an achievement carried on through his sons Sir George Christie and Gus Christie.

Bearers of the Christie name have also excelled in the creative world of the written word, no less so than the British crime writer **Agatha Christie**, whose books are still best-sellers more than 35 years after her death in 1976.

Born Agatha Mary Clarissa Miller in Torquay, Devon, in 1890, she took the Christie surname after marrying the Royal Flying Corps pilot Archie Christie shortly after the outbreak of the First World War in 1914.

Her first novel, *The Mysterious Affair at Styles*, was published in 1920, and although she also wrote romance novels under the pen-name of Mary Westmacott, it is for her 80 crime novels, featuring either Miss Jane Marple or the Belgian detective Hercule Poirot, that she is best known.

Many of these, such as *Death on the Nile*,

Murder on the Orient Express, *Murder at the Vicarage* and *Evil Under the Sun* have been the subject of numerous television and film adaptations, while her stage play *The Mousetrap* retains the record for the longest theatre run.

First opening in London in November of 1952, as of 2011 it is still packing in audiences after more than 23,000 performances.

Christie herself became the subject of a mystery worthy of one of her own novels in December of 1926.

This was when she disappeared from her marital home in Berkshire. After eleven days she was traced to a hotel in Harrogate, Yorkshire, signed in under an assumed name.

Christie never gave any public explanation for her disappearance, although it is widely accepted that she may have had suffered a breakdown after her husband told her he wanted a divorce.

The couple did indeed divorce, two years later, and the writer later married the British archaeologist Max Mallowan.

Made a Dame Commander of the Order of the British Empire in 1971, Christie is listed in the Guinness Book of World Records as the best-selling author of all time and the most translated individual author.

In contemporary times, **Evie Christie**, born in 1979, is the Canadian poet and writer whose works include her 2005 poetry collection *Gutted* and the 2010 novel *The Bourgeois Empire*.

In the highly competitive world of sport, **Linford Christie**, born in 1960 in Saint Andrew, Jamaica, and settling at the age of seven with his family in Acton, London, is the former world champion sprinter who is now a successful athletics coach.

His many achievements on the track include winning no less than seven gold medals in the 100-metres event – at the 1992 Olympic Games, the 1993 World Championships, the European Championships in 1986, 1990 and 1994 and the Commonwealth Games in both 1990 and 1994.

Also the holder of three gold medals for the European Indoor Championships, his track career ended in 1999, when he received a two-year ban for allegedly having taken a performance-enhancing substance – a claim that the former athlete has vociferously and persistently denied.

Awarded an MBE in 1990, named BBC Sports Personality of the Year in 1993 and awarded an

OBE in 1998, he has since successfully coached British athletes Darren Campbell and Katharine Merry towards Olympic medals.

From athletics to the rough and tumble that is the sport of rugby union, George Christie, better known as **Kitch Christie**, was the South African player and coach who was born in Johannesburg in 1940 to a Scottish father and an English mother.

A flanker with the Pretoria Harlequins, he later made his name as coach of the South African national team, the Springboks, helping to lead it to victory in the 1995 Rugby World Cup; he died in 1998.

One of the most evil bearers of the otherwise proud name of Christie was the British serial killer **John Christie**, known to have murdered at least six women, including his wife, between 1943 and 1953.

Born in 1899 in Halifax, West Yorkshire, and having married and settled by the outbreak of the Second World War in a flat at 10 Rillington Place, in the Notting Hill area of London, Christie had a string of previous convictions for assault and theft – but police failed to check this before accepting him for Special Constable duties.

It was not until he moved out of 10 Rillington Place in March of 1953 that new tenants discovered the bodies of three of his victims hidden in a kitchen alcove, while others were later discovered buried in a backyard and hidden in a wash-house.

One of the bodies was identified as that of his wife, Ethel, and it was for her murder that he was hanged in July of 1953.

It subsequently emerged that his victims – some sources assert there may have been as many as eight – were usually strangled by Christie in his flat after he had rendered them unconscious by administering domestic gas and, in some cases, raping them.

In a controversy that persists to this day, Christie had been a key prosecution witness three years before his own trial in the trial for murder of Timothy Evans.

Evans and his wife, Beryl, had been tenants of Christie during 1948 and 1949, and Evans was hanged after being found guilty of his infant daughter's murder.

In what was a complex case, he had also been charged with his wife's murder, but the jury did not find sufficient evidence to convict him of this.

With the subsequent conviction for murder of Christie, it became apparent that Evans had not been guilty of any murder and, as a consequence, was granted a posthumous pardon in October of 1966.

The miscarriage of justice involving Evans is considered to have significantly contributed a year before his pardon to the abolition of capital punishment for murder in the United Kingdom.

Richard Attenborough later chillingly portrayed Christie in the 1977 film *10 Rillington Place*, based in part on the book of the same name by the late campaigning journalist and author Ludovic Kennedy.

On a much more uplifting note, **Fyffe Christie**, born in 1918 in Bushey, Hertfordshire, to a Scots father and an English mother, was a noted figurative artist and mural painter.

It was following the death of his mother in 1930 that he settled in Glasgow, where his father, George Fyffe Christie, established a successful career as an artist – creating and sketching the popular character "Scottikins" for the local *Bulletin* newspaper.

Burning with ambition to also pursue an artistic career, Fyffe Christie was handicapped by the fact that he suffered from an extreme form of dyslexia, and it was not until he was a young teenager that he was able to read, albeit after a fashion.

In common with many others who have suffered from the affliction of dyslexia, Christie eventually managed to surmount it and go on to pursue a very successful career.

An accomplished musician, he served as a piper with the British Army during the Second World War, at the end of which conflict he enrolled as a student at the Glasgow School of Art, specialising in mural painting.

The outcome was a series of stunning and enduring murals that, before his death in 1979, included ones for the Glasgow School of Piping and Glasgow University Union.

His particularly noted *Christ Feeding the People*, originally executed for the Iona Community in Glasgow's Clyde Street, is now in the careful care of a private collector.